SCHIRMER
PERFORMANCE
EDITIONS

THE BAROQUE ERA
Intermediate Level

Compiled and Edited by Richard Walters

AUDIO ACCESS INCLUDED
Recorded Performances Online

Recorded by

Elena Abend
Matthew Edwards
Stefanie Jacob
Christos Tsitsaros
Jeannie Yu

To access companion recorded performances online, visit:
www.halleonard.com/mylibrary

Enter Code
7948-2291-7570-4954

On the cover:
St. Cecilia and the Angel (c. 1610)
by Carlo Saraceni (1579–1620)

ISBN 978-1-4803-3819-7

G. SCHIRMER, Inc.

DISTRIBUTED BY
HAL•LEONARD®
CORPORATION
7777 W. BLUEMOUND RD. P.O. BOX 13819 MILWAUKEE, WI 53213

Copyright © 2014 by G. Schirmer, Inc. (ASCAP) New York, NY
International Copyright Secured. All Rights Reserved.

Warning: Unauthorized reproduction of this publication is
prohibited by Federal law and subject to criminal prosecution.

www.musicsalesclassical.com
www.halleonard.com

CONTENTS

Though the table of contents appears in alphabetical order by composer, the music in this book is in progressive order.

The price of this publication includes access to companion recorded performances online, for download or streaming, using the unique code found on the title page. Visit **www.halleonard.com/mylibrary** and enter the access code.

The music in this collection has been edited by the compiler/editor Richard Walters, except for the pieces previously published in other volumes in the Schirmer Performance Editions series:

Anonymous: Polonaise, BWV App. 119
from *First Lessons in Bach*
edited and recorded by Christos Tsitsaros

Anonymous: Minuet, BWV App. 120
from *Selections from the Notebook for Anna Magdelena Bach*
edited and recorded by Christos Tsitsaros

C.P.E. Bach: March, BWV App. 124
from *First Lessons in Bach*
edited and recorded by Christos Tsitsaros

J. S. Bach: Prelude, BWV 926; Prelude, BWV 927; Prelude, BWV 999
from *Nineteen Little Preludes*
edited and recorded by Christos Tsitsaros

J. S. Bach: Bourrée, BWV 996
from *First Lessons in Bach*
edited and recorded by Christos Tsitsaros

COMPOSER BIOGRAPHIES
AND
PERFORMANCE NOTES

General Comments about the Baroque Era and This Edition

As is the case with many Baroque pieces, we often do not have dynamics and articulations from the original composer. This music was not written with a modern piano in mind. The harpsichord and claviers of the period were not capable of dynamic variation in the manner of a modern piano. When playing Baroque music on the piano it is only natural to add dynamic contrasts, which makes it more idiomatic for the modern instrument. Dynamics and articulations have been added as editorial suggestions in many instances.

Minuet is traditionally spelled differently, depending on the language. For this edition we have chosen to use the traditional English spelling "minuet." One might encounter some of the minuets in this collection elsewhere with various spellings in various languages: Minuet (English); Minuetto (Italian); Menuet (French); Menuett (German).

A minuet was a dance movement, originating in France, usually in 3/4 meter, popular in the period between 1650–1800. It has regular four measure phrases and is in binary form. In a classic minuet that is to be danced, the second beat of the measure is accented. However, composers do not always observe this. Minuets became concert music inspired by dance music, but not intended for dancing. The minuet was one of the only Baroque dance music forms that survived into the Classical Era.

In the Baroque period, ornamentation is part of the style and was historically added by players in the performance. In this edition intended for students, we have been very discreet in any ornament suggestions. However, a teacher might guide a student in adding ornamentation. Ornamentation can be heard sometimes on the companion recording which may be used as a guide.

A constantly applied *legato* touch, common to piano playing after the Romantic period, is not appropriate to music of the Baroque and Classical periods. *Legato* playing should be deliberately chosen only for specific places, such as the notes included in a slur, not generally applied as a default. Style in the Baroque period comes from maintaining steady rhythm, a crisp touch with careful attention to articulation, the general avoidance of the sustaining pedal, and period ornamentation. In most instances a slightly separated touch, *portato*, should be applied when no articulation is indicated.

Because the notes below are likely to be read one piece at a time as needed, many concepts applying generally to playing Baroque period music are restated many times.

ANONYMOUS

Johann Sebastian Bach included the following pieces (BWV Appendix 119 and 120) in the second volume, dated 1725, of the *Notebook for Anna Magdalena Bach*. The notebooks (the first was begun in 1722) were for Bach's second wife, Anna Magdalena, who was much younger than the composer. Such keyboard notebooks of assembled favorite pieces were common in Baroque homes, and used for family music-making. (They are the equivalent of the modern published music collection, such as this one.) Some of the pieces in the Anna Magdalena notebook are by J.S. Bach; others are not. Previously attributed to Bach, we now know that the pieces below are not J.S. Bach compositions. The composers are unknown. We can assume that they date from the first decades of the eighteenth century are likely German in origin.

Polonaise in G minor, BWV Appendix 119
A polonaise stems from Polish folk dances. The term began to be used in the seventeenth century primarily by composers outside Poland. Originally a vocal form, by the time of Bach it had become an instrumental form characterized by triple meter and short repeated sections. The polonaise was later developed in the Romantic period, notably by Chopin. The composer of

this polonaise is unknown, previously attributed to J. S. Bach. Articulation is crucial in bringing to life any style of music. Articulation has been editorially suggested in this edition to help achieve a Baroque style. Notice frequent use of the *staccato* combined with a *tenuto* marking, indicating a slight separation between notes. Slurs are brief groupings of notes to be played *legato*. Do not make the mistake of applying a *legato* touch as the norm in Baroque music. It should be thought of as a choice to be made deliberately and only in specific places. *Staccato* markings are also used on eighth notes in this piece. Dynamics are editorial suggestions. Remember in this period, the instrument this music was written for, likely a harpsichord, did not have the capabilities of a modern piano. Ornamentation is possible in this style. We have noted two places where a trill is optional. You can hear this ornamentation on the companion recording.

Minuet in A minor, BWV Appendix 120
This minuet was previously attributed to J.S. Bach. Further research has discovered that it is in fact not by Bach; the composer is unknown. It has a contemplative quality, unusual for a minuet. This piece is in two large, obvious sections, both repeated. The character of the music remains fairly constant throughout, but there is more harmonic tension and use of ornaments at the end of the second section. A few slurs of brief notes to be played *legato* have been indicated as editorial suggestions. The general touch for this piece might be described as *portato*, which is a slightly detached touch. Trills begin on the note above in every case. Some pianists will find the left hand trills in measures 22 and 24 particularly challenging. If these cannot be gracefully mastered, one might play the right hand trills only. Notice that the pianist on the companion recording also adds additional ornamentation on the repeat of both sections, which is stylistically appropriate for the Baroque. The composer has given no tempo. The recorded performance is a good guide. We caution you not to take this piece too slowly. Pedal probably should be avoided.

CARL PHILIPP EMANUEL BACH
German composer.
Born in Weimar, March 8, 1714;
died in Hamburg, December 14, 1788.

Carl Philipp Emanuel Bach, second son of Johann Sebastian Bach, was a major composer bridging the distinctions between late Baroque and early Classical periods, writing in the *empfindsamer Stil* (sensitive style), meaning an emotionally turbulent or dynamically expressive compositional style, as distinguished from the more restrained rococo. Carl received music lessons from his father until he began studies in law at Leipzig University and continued in Frankfurt. After graduation, C.P.E. Bach accepted a position in the court orchestra of Crown Prince Frederick of Prussia and moved to Berlin. In 1768 C.P.E. Bach became the music director of sacred music for the city of Hamburg, a position previously held by his godfather, Georg Philipp Telemann. C.P. E. Bach was extraordinarily prolific, writing over 1,000 works for voices and keyboard instruments.

March in G Major, BWV Appendix 124
This march, included in the second volume of the *Notebook for Anna Magdalena Bach*, is usually attributed to Carl Philipp Emmanuel Bach. A march is generally in 2/2 meter as is this one. A march needs a very steady beat. When deciding on a tempo for a march, imagine a walking tempo. This march is a rather fast walk. Tempo should remain very steady. We have made editorial suggestions regarding articulation and dynamics which will bring the style of the piece to life. Pay careful notice to which notes are indicated to be played *legato* with slurs, which notes are short *staccato*, and which notes are to be played with slight separation, indicated by a *staccato* marking combined with a *tenuto* marking. The trills in measures 7 and 20 should begin on the note above. The *arpeggios* in measures 8 and 21 have a military flavor. Do not use pedal in playing this march. The form is a simple AB, with both sections repeated.

JOHANN SEBASTIAN BACH
German composer and organist.
Born in Eisenach, March 21, 1685;
died in Leipzig, July 28, 1750.

One of the greatest composers in the history of music, J. S. Bach defined the high Baroque style, developing counterpoint in composition further than any composer before him or since. However, during his lifetime he was more known for his virtuoso keyboard playing than for composition. The modern recognition of Bach as a master composer began in the mid-nineteenth century, decades after his death. Throughout his life Bach wrote keyboard music for his students, including his children. As a church organist for most of his life, Bach would often improvise preludes to various services. Occasionally these improvisations were written down and formalized into keyboard pieces for Bach's students or for publication. Bach composed hundreds of works, most for practical occasions, including cantatas, oratorios, motets, various instrumental suites, harpsichord works, organ works, and orchestral pieces. He came from a long line of musicians, and was father to six noted composers.

Prelude in D minor BWV 926

Bach gave us no tempo marking for this piece. However, there is a clue as to what your individual tempo should be. Look at the fast moving sixteenth notes in measures 39–42. The performance tempo at which you ultimately arrive is determined by how well you can master these measures. You cannot suddenly slow down to accommodate the fast-moving sixteenth notes. This is a common problem in piano music. One section is much more difficult than the rest of the piece, and is the determining factor when choosing a tempo. The good performance on the companion recording may be faster than a student pianist can master. It's perfectly acceptable to play the prelude at a slower tempo. This edition includes Bach's original few markings regarding articulation, notably the *legato* slurs in measures 9–10 and 13–14. Other than this, Bach gave us no articulation. Performance practice during the period would have taken care of other articulation expected in the piece. Instead, you must apply stylistic knowledge. We hesitate to add a lot of editorially suggested articulation in an edition of Bach. We would rather advise you about particular points. The quarter notes which appear in the left hand in measures 10, 14, and 20–38 should be played with slight separation. Likewise, the moving eighth notes in the right hand, except when marked by Bach with slurs as *legato*, should also be played with a slight separation. If you play the entire piece with *legato* touch, which is the default thinking for many pianists, you will completely miss the Baroque style. Ornamentation is open for interpretation. The mordent which appears on the downbeat of measure 1 in the left hand may be played either beginning on the beat, or, as the pianist on the companion recording, beginning slightly before the beat. This is an interpretive choice in Baroque music of moderate to fast tempo. In a slower tempo, a mordent such as this would always begin on the beat. One must achieve supreme evenness and steadiness when playing Bach. You will need to practice hands separately at a slow tempo. During this slow practice is when you confirm your decisions about fingering and articulation. Then practice at a slow tempo hands together. It can help some pianists to break the piece down into short sections for practice, rather than continually practicing the piece the entire way through. The sixteenth notes in measures 39–42 are a quasi-toccata moment. When a line such as this is passed from hand to hand, the listener's ear should notice no difference in the sound.

Prelude in F Major, BWV 927

Notice that there are no *legato* slurs anywhere in this piece. All eight notes, including the diads in measures 1–4, should be played with slight separation. This also applies to the single eighth notes in the left hand in measures 5–8 and other places. Perpetual motion of sixteenth notes is common in Bach. You must achieve absolute steadiness and evenness. The tempo cannot waiver anyplace in this piece except at the end, as indicated. You must practice hands alone, slowly. Then practice hands together, slowly. Allow the music to come into you muscle memory over time at a slow tempo. Do not proceed into a quicker tempo prematurely in your practice. Only practice this piece at a tempo at which you can keep the entire composition at a steady pace. Pedal should not be used in this prelude. The ending in measures 14 and 15 is reminiscent of a toccata, a sudden bit of freedom breaking up the mood and pattern of the piece. The Alberti figure of sixteenth notes, in places such as the right hand in measures 1–2 and left hand measures 3–4, must be mastered. We suggest practicing these sixteenth note figures in several different ways. Practice first deliberately with athletic finger movement. Then follow that by practicing with a much lighter touch.

Bourrée
from Lute Suite No. 1 in E minor, BWV 996

A bourrée is a lively dance movement, French in origin from the Baroque always in 2/2 or 4/4 meter, and in binary form. A bourrée always begins with a quarter note upbeat. A bourrée became an optional part of the standard Baroque suite. Though the bourrée fell out of favor after the Baroque period among composers, the original folk dance is still found in the Auvergne region of France. There is no tempo indication in Bach's manuscript. In keeping with a traditional bourée, we have suggested *Allegro moderato*. Bach indicated no dynamics or articulations in his manuscript. There are editorial suggestions about these details which will help create appropriate Baroque style.

Note that the quarter notes in the left hand should be played detached throughout, not as short as *staccato*. Imagine these quarter notes to be eighth notes followed by eighth note rests. It may be obvious, but in the bass clef, notes that are up-stemmed are to be played with the right hand. As is true in all Baroque music, you should play with a very steady tempo. Practice should begin slowly, hands alone. In this hands alone practice, you should confirm the fingering you chose and also apply articulation from the beginning of practice. Then practice hands together, slowly continuing to use deliberate fingering and articulation. Use no pedal in playing this bourrée.

Prelude in C minor, BWV 999

Bach almost always creates a tight composition with rhythmic structure. This piece uses the same rhythmic structure throughout except in the last two measures. Because the hands are so rhythmically integrated, it is probably best not to practice this piece hands alone, but rather practice hands together slowly. A few stylistic pointers for the left hand are in order. Notice that the downbeat is a quarter followed by a rest. Do not hold this note longer than its quarter-note value. The eighth notes on beat 3 should be played *staccato* throughout. The quarter note that follows the eighth notes should not be *staccato*. The sixteenth notes in the right hand must be played evenly throughout. The harmonic movement is the propelling factor in this piece, with the harmony changing for each measure. If you would like to see the harmonic progression Bach has created, you can play all of the notes in any measure together as a chord. Do not use pedal in this piece. There should be no variation in tempo. The only place this is allowed is in the penultimate measure. You should practice this piece at a slow tempo and gradually over time increase you practice tempo, but never play this faster than you can maintain as a steady tempo throughout. There should be calmness to your performance even though the music is quite busy.

FRANÇOIS COUPERIN

French composer, harpsichordist, and organist.
Born in Paris, November 10, 1668;
died in Paris, September 11, 1733.

François was the son of the organist at Saint Gervais church in Paris. His father died when the boy was ten. Saint Gervais not only saved his father's position for the budding young musician and paid for his musical education, the church also paid for the housing and upkeep of François and his mother until he was old enough to assume the duties as full-time organist in 1688. In this period the royal court controlled all copyrights. Couperin obtained permission to publish his music. He was appointed organist of the King in 1693 and began teaching harpsichord to much of Parisian aristocracy. For the rest of his life he was regarded as one of the greatest teachers and keyboard players in France. Couperin published four books of harpsichord pieces, considered as landmarks of the French Baroque style. He was the author of a definitive treatise, *The Art of Harpsichord Playing*, addressing fingering, touch, ornamentation and various other aspects of keyboard technique.

The Little Trifle (Le Petit-Rien)
from the fourteenth order of Harpsichord Pieces

This piece has the perfect structure of a simple rondo. A rondo (rondeau) is music with a recurring theme, with other musical material in between theme statements. The theme is measures 1–16. This recurs in measures 25–40 and 59–74. The couplets present different music, related to the theme by motive. The composer has given us a marking of *légérement*, which means lightly, but does not address tempo. The admirable tempo on the companion recording may be too fast for some students. A slower tempo is acceptable. Whatever tempo you choose, make sure the piece is played with lightness and steadiness. The Baroque style in France was different from the familiar German style of Bach and the Italian style of Scarlatti. French Baroque music is often much more heavily ornamented. We suggest that if you find the ornamentation challenging, you might attempt to play only the right hand ornaments and omit the left hand ornaments. Articulation needs to be carefully considered. We have suggested staccatos on eighth notes such as in measure 1, which is part of the style and will help achieve the lightness that Couperin has requested. Notice the suggested two-note slurs on the sixteenth notes such as in measures 2, 4, and 5. The sixteenth notes for a full measure, such as measures 18, 19, 22, and 23 can be played one of two ways. If your tempo is a quick one, they will probably be played slurred. If your tempo is not quite so fast, these running sixteenth notes can also be played with slight detachment in this style. This happy music needs to be played with a light spirit and a light touch. Clarity is your aim. Any pedal will smear the music and undermine that intention.

JEAN-FRANÇOIS DANDRIEU
French composer and organist.
Born in Paris, 1681 (or 1682);
died in Paris January 17, 1738.

Dandrieu became organist at St. Merry in Paris in 1704. He had established himself prior to this as a competent keyboard player. The composer was also the organist for St. Barthélemy and the royal chapel. He is remembered today for his books of harpsichord pieces, which capture the French Baroque style most similar to that of Couperin.

Lament (La Gémissante)
from the second suite of Harpsichord Pieces, Book 1
This is a delicate lament in the treble range of the piano and it requires a refined, delicate touch. The composer has indicated that the piece should be played tenderly. The musical structure is essentially a rondo. The theme is measures 1–16. This recurs in measures 26–41 and 50–65. The musical material changes between these statements of the theme. We might recommend that the repeat of the first section be omitted. Even though the music moves along, it has a sad spirit to it that the performer needs to capture. Essentially this is a song-like melody in the right hand, with a left hand supporting figure that answers the right hand. Therefore, the right hand melody should be slightly more pronounced. We have also recommended articulation that makes the slurring different in the right hand melody from the accompaniment figure in the left hand. Unlike most Baroque music, this particular piece may benefit from discreet use of the sustaining pedal, but it must be used with subtlety and remain inconspicuous.

GEORGE FRIDERIC HANDEL
German composer.
Born in Halle, February 23, 1685;
died in London, April 14, 1759.

Handel was one of the defining composers of the Baroque period. After a brief time in Italy as a young man, he spent nearly his entire adult career in London, where he became famous as a composer of opera and oratorio, including *Messiah*, now his most recognizable music. Handel also wrote numerous concertos, suites, overtures, cantatas, trio sonatas, and solo keyboard works. Though he taught some students early in his career and occasionally instructed members of the London aristocracy, Handel was not known for his teaching abilities. His keyboard works were likely not written for any of his students, but to fulfill commissions or generate income. Handel composed various keyboard works until 1720, when he became master of the orchestra for the Royal Academy of Music, an organization dedicated to performing new operas. After Italian opera fell out of vogue in London, Handel turned his compositional efforts to oratorio.

Allegro from Suite in G minor, HWV 432
Like many faster Baroque keyboard pieces, this movement is about maintaining steadiness throughout. All the sixteenth notes, which are constantly present, need to be played with evenness and steadiness. You will need to practice hands alone at a slow tempo at early stages of learning the piece. Only move to a faster tempo in your practice when you can maintain it steadily. This particular piece, and many others in the Baroque like it, is not much about dynamic contrasts. You must find a touch that is appropriate to this music which sounds buoyant and nimble. We have made stylistic suggestion about articulation of eighth notes, which should be played with slight separation. Even though the music is quite busy, a good performance of it, such as the one on the companion recording, ultimately has a sense of calm about it. The admirable tempo on the recording may not be attainable by all pianists. Find a tempo at which you can keep the music steady and even.

Prelude in G Major
from *Suite de pièce*, Volume 2, No. 9, HWV 442
Articulation and steadiness are the key factors in this prelude. We have suggested that some eighth notes be played staccato, and some in two-note slurs, which will create appropriate style. The quarter notes should be played slightly detached. At an *allegro* tempo, the sixteenth notes by default will be played slurred. However, they are usually not marked as such and we have not marked them here. Your touch should be light, refined, and elegant. You must practice first hands alone at a slow tempo, incorporating articulation in the early stages of learning the piece. Move on to hands together, practicing slowly, retaining the articulations you have learned while practicing hands alone. Over several weeks of practice you will increase the speed of your playing only at the pace at which you can keep a steady beat. Don't forget the joyous nature of this prelude. It should not sound labored.

JOHANN PHILIPP KIRNBERGER

German theorist and composer.
Born in Saalfeld, April 24, 1721;
died in Berlin, July 26 (or 27), 1783.

A student of J. S. Bach, Kirnberger was a life-long champion of the great composer, spending much of his life accumulating and ensuring the continued publication of Bach's music. Apart from composition, Kirnberger was also a theorist, inventing several alternate methods of tempering the tuning of a keyboard instrument. He held several court and church appointments throughout Germany and Poland, including the Chapel of Prince Heinrich of Prussia and Princess Anna Amalia.

The Chimes (Les Carillons)

This happy piece is in two large sections with the first section repeated, requiring a lightness of touch, crisp articulation, and steadiness in playing. This piece needs a refined, elegant tone from the pianist. In practicing hands alone slowly, make sure that you are not only learning the correct notes and rhythms but also, from the early stages, are learning articulation, so that it becomes and organic part of your performance. Articulation is not like a cake decoration to be added after the cake is baked. Clarity is your aim. Thus, do not use pedal. Notice that we have suggested playing the quarter notes detached. *Legato* touch is only applied in short slurred phrases of a few notes. There should be a slight lift when moving from one slurred figure to another, such as moving from beat 3 to 4 in the right hand of measure 3. The alternative section on the second page has a playful mystery about it, as if the composer is taking us down some delightfully interesting new path. When you go back to the beginning, do not play the repeats.

PIETRO DOMENICO PARADIES [PARADISI]

Italian composer and teacher.
Born in Naples, 1707;
died in Venice, August 25, 1791.

Paradisi (his original name) spent many unsuccessful years in Italy, attempting to establish himself as an opera composer. Failed stage works in Naples and Venice caused him to seek employment in London, where he changed his name to Paradies, as a teacher and composer of harpsichord music. He later moved back to Italy to retire. Though his vocal works never gained the notoriety he wished, his *Twelve Sonatas for Gravicembalo* (a predecessor to the piano) became extremely popular during his life and into the next century. The second movement of the sixth sonata is a perennial favorite of student pianists today, often published separately as "Toccata."

Toccata from Sonata No. 6 in A Major

A toccata is a brilliant composition showing virtuoso playing. This toccata is driven by relentless sixteenth notes. The greatest challenge is to master steadiness and evenness from start to finish. Any student pianist will need to practice hands alone slowly. The right hand particularly needs much slow practice. Because it is a lengthy piece, your practice should be divided into short sections. The eighth notes of the left hand, primarily, should be played detached throughout. In your practice you should gradually increase your speed as you master the music. Your ultimate tempo can only be as fast as you can manage. If you don't achieve the tempo of the companion recorded performance, do not be concerned. Just be sure the tempo you choose is steady and one that sounds controlled and is not running away from you. Many student pianists make the mistake of speeding up in quick moving music. This toccata is not really about dynamic contrasts, and we have not suggested any. This piece will make its impact purely through even playing from start to finish.

JEAN-PHILIPPE RAMEAU

French composer and theorist.
Born in Dijon, September 25, 1683;
died in Paris, September 12, 1764.

Rameau studied with his father, an organist, before continuing his music education in Italy. He returned to France as a violinist in a traveling music troupe and then became organist at Clermont Cathedral. By 1706, Rameau was in Paris serving in various places as organist and publishing his first keyboard works. After a few brief appointments as organist in Dijon and Lyons, Rameau returned to Paris permanently. He published his most famous theoretical work, *Traité de l'harmonie*, in 1722. Late in life, the composer took up writing operas. Rameau is remembered as one of the most influential composers of keyboard music of the French Baroque.

Tambourin from Harpsichord Pieces

A tambourin is a drum from the Provence region of France. In the eighteenth century, a French dance invented for the theatre was based on this drum. A tambourin has bass notes that are pedal tones (the

E-minor harmony), an oboe-like melody and duple meter. We have no tempo marking from Rameau. We have suggested *moderato*, which allows for a wide range of choices. One can imagine a tempo at a slower pace than that on the companion recorded as an acceptable choice. In fact, a slower moderato might help some pianists in adding the ornamentation which is so intrinsic to the style. Note that the trills begin on the note above. This music has a strong rhythmic feel appropriate to a dance movement. Your performance should capture the rhythmic energy and remain at an absolutely steady tempo throughout. The composer provided no articulation or dynamics. We have made articulation suggestions that reflect the French Baroque style. Dynamics are much more subjective and there are many possibilities. Our choice was to recommend a strong beginning and a quiet ending. There are other acceptable possibilities regarding dynamics. Use no pedal in this piece.

DOMENICO SCARLATTI
Italian composer and harpsichordist.
Born in Naples, October 26, 1685;
died in Madrid, July 23, 1757.

Domenico was one of two musical sons of Alessandro Scarlatti. Domenico was extraordinarily influential in the development of solo keyboard music, composing nearly 600 sonatas for the instrument. He was taught by his father and other musicians in Naples until he secured the position of composer and organist for the royal chapel in Naples at the age of 15. He spent time in Venice and Rome serving as the Maestro di cappella at St. Peter's before moving to Lisbon, where he taught the Portuguese Princess. In 1728, he moved to Spain where he would spend the rest of his life, finally settling in Madrid. In Madrid he was the music master for the Princess and later Queen of Spain.

A sonata in the Baroque period is different from its mature development in the Classical Era. A sonata in the Baroque almost always meant a one-movement piece. Its musical form was not defined and could be many possibilities. The word sonata was used in Italy for instrumental works. The Italian Baroque style is distinctly different from the German Baroque style and the French Baroque style. Without going into complicated detail, the Italian Baroque style had more freedom than its German counterpart. Domenico Scarlatti wrote over 500 keyboard sonatas. These are some of the easiest of his sonatas.

Sonata in G Major, L. 79 (K. 391, P. 364)
This is stylish music and requires style in playing. Our editorial suggestions indicate some stylistic qualities of the period, such as quarter notes that are played with slight separation (marked with a *staccato* combined with a *tenuto*). Scarlatti's music often has a playful quality, and we have indicated dynamics which differ upon repeated sections to help create this playfulness. Trills begin on the note above in this period. The *acciaccatura*, which appears on the downbeat of measure 11, is to be played quickly with the principle note on the beat. The piece in general requires a light touch and great clarity. No pedal should be used.

Sonata in D minor, L. 423 (K. 32, P. 14)
A characteristic of the Baroque Era is beautiful, contemplative minor key compositions such as this one. This aria, closely related to vocal music, has a particular brand of Baroque melancholy. However, do not make the piece so expressive that it becomes played as if in the Romantic Era. The thirty-second notes which appear many places are written out ornaments in this edition. You will succeed in making the melody in the right hand expressive by working at the articulation of the melody. We have made stylistic suggestions about which notes should be slurred (meaning that the notes in the slurred group are played *legato*) and which should be played *staccato*. The short two-note and three-note slurs are a Baroque characteristic indicating weeping. We can imagine a tempo that would be slightly slower than the recorded performance, however, we caution you not to play this sonata too slowly. A small *rit.* before heading into the *fine* is appropriate.

GEORG PHILIPP TELEMANN
German composer.
Born in Magdeburg, March 14, 1681;
died in Hamburg, June 25, 1767.

A prominent German Baroque composer, Telemann was instrumental in expanding figured bass composition and defining Baroque ornamentation. He is sometimes cited as the most prolific composer who ever lived, with over 3,000 known music works, including about 150 keyboard pieces. He also wrote and published poetry. Telemann was a self-taught musician who held a series of positions in Leipzig, Sorau, Eisenach, Frankfurt, and finally Hamburg, where he became the music director of the city's churches.

Dance Suite No. 2 in F Major

Suites became popular forms of compositions in the Baroque period. The number of movements in a suite varied quite a bit. The instrumental Baroque suites were generally based on dance forms.

Movement I: A gavotte is a Baroque dance movement in duple meter with regular four-measure phrases that begin in the middle of the measure. A gavotte is also characterized by simple rhythms and generally avoids syncopation. However, Telemann's gavotte does use some syncopation. A gavotte is a graceful dance, and this music should be played with a refined touch. We have suggested in this edition that the left hand quarter notes should be played with slight detachment throughout. The right hand melody needs to be played with stylish articulation. We have suggested which notes should be played *staccato* and which should be played in short slurs. A fun aspect of the piece is the composer's move to the minor key for the middle section (measure 20). If the movement feels too long to you, you could consider omitting the repeats. The repeats should certainly be omitted in the *da capo*. No pedal should be used in this gavotte.

Movement II: Sarabande has its roots in the Zarabanda, a fast and erotic dance from Mexico and Spain in the sixteenth century. In France, this was transformed into a slow Baroque dance, essentially a slow minuet that was highly expressive. Baroque sarabandes tend to be majestic or mournful and are characterized by a dotted note on the second beat. Notice that the left hand quarter notes in this movement are often to be played with suggested slurs, contrasting to the detached quarter notes in the gavotte. The melody in the right hand should have a singing quality about it. Trills begin on the note above. In slower Baroque movements, a stylistic choice might be to begin the trills slowly and speed up, but do not exaggerate this if you choose to do it. Tempo is always open to interpretation. One can imagine a tempo that is faster than on the companion recording.

Movement III. A bourrée is a lively dance movement, French in origin from the Baroque, always in 2/2 or 4/4 meter, and in binary form. A bourrée always begins with a quarter note upbeat. A bourrée became an optional part of the standard Baroque suite. Though the bourrée fell out of favor after the Baroque period among composers, but the original folk dance is still around in the Auvergne region of France. This lively bourrée will become

stylish if you pay close attention to articulation. We suggest that you learn articulation from the beginning, in the early stages of learning the piece, when practicing hands alone slowly. When you begin to practice slowly, hands together, then you will have already added articulation as an organic part of the music. This movement needs a light touch, elegant tone, and no pedal. Tempo needs to be very steady throughout.

Cantabile in F Major

The word cantabile means singing. In this case the composer means that the melody should be played with a singing tone. The left hand is the accompaniment that keeps the beat steady and disciplines the melody. The left hand quarter notes should be played slightly detached throughout. On top of this, the right hand achieves its expressiveness through thoughtful articulation. *Andante* is a tempo that can be interpreted in various ways. One can imagine a tempo at a quicker pace than is on the companion recording, but don't take the piece too quickly. This elegant melody needs a refined touch.

—Richard Walters, editor
Joshua Parman, assistant editor

Polonaise in G minor

Composer unknown
BWV Appendix 119

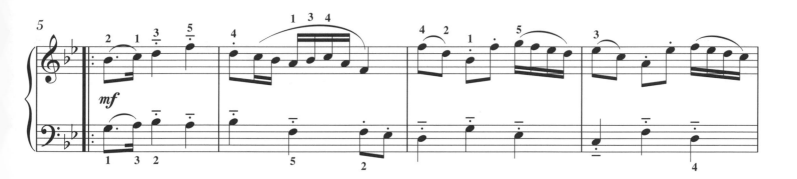

Fingering by Christos Tsitsaros.
*These wedge markings in the right hand, indicating marcato, appear in the source manuscript. Other articulations, tempo and dynamics are editorial suggestions.

Copyright © 2009 by G. Schirmer, Inc. (ASCAP), New York, NY
International Copyright Secured. All Rights Reserved.

Minuet in A minor

Composer unknown
BWV Appendix 120

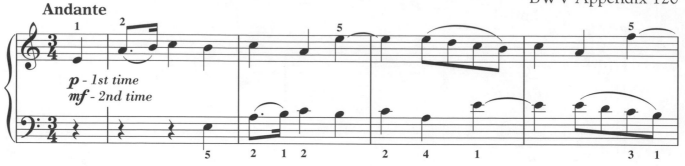

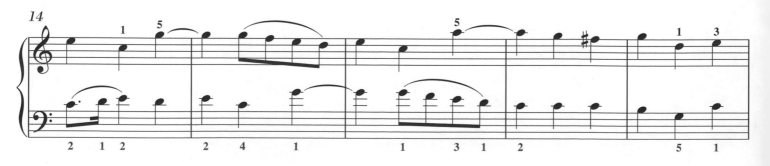

Fingering by Christos Tsitsaros.
Tempo, articulations, and dynamics are editorial suggestions.

Copyright © 2005 by G. Schirmer, Inc. (ASCAP) New York, NY
International Copyright Secured. All Rights Reserved.

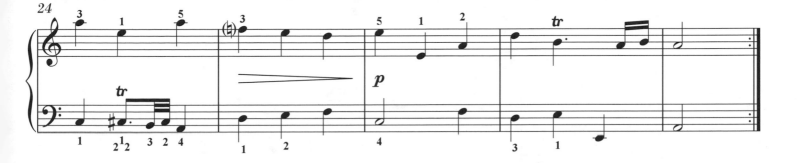

The Chimes
(Les Carillons)

Johann Philipp Kirnberger

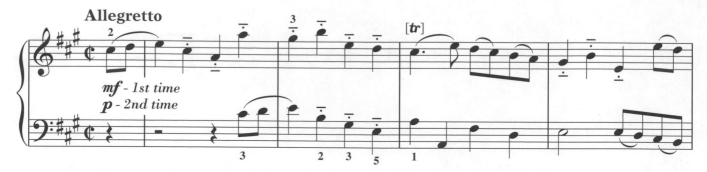

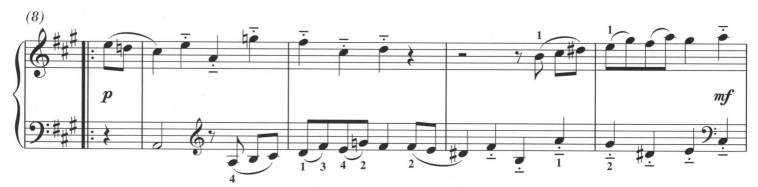

Fingering by Stefanie Jacob.
Tempo, articulations and dynamics are stylistic editorial suggestions. Trills begin on the note above.
No repeats on the *Da Capo*.

Copyright © 2014 by G. Schirmer, Inc. (ASCAP) New York, NY
International Copyright Secured. All Rights Reserved.

ALTERNATIVO

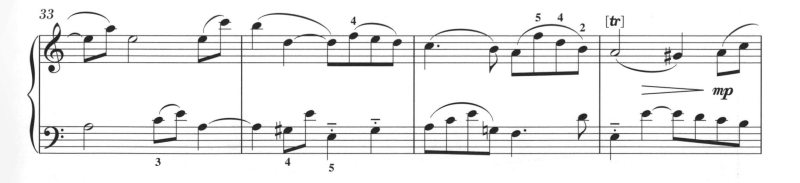

D.C. al Fine

March in G Major

Carl Philipp Emanuel Bach
BWV Appendix 124

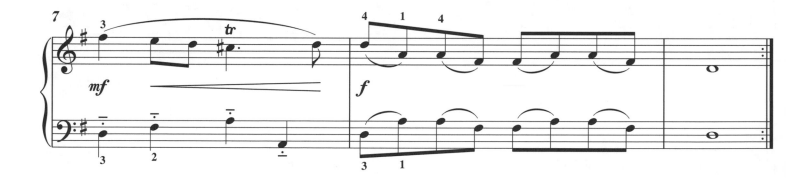

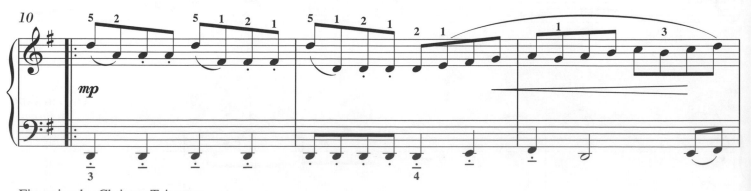

Fingering by Christos Tsitsaros.
Tempo, articulations, and dynamics are editorial suggestions.

Copyright © 2009 by G. Schirmer, Inc. (ASCAP), New York, NY
International Copyright Secured. All Rights Reserved.

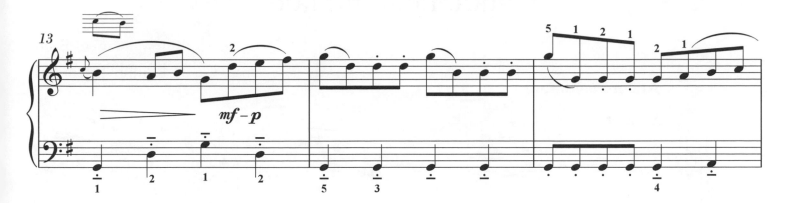

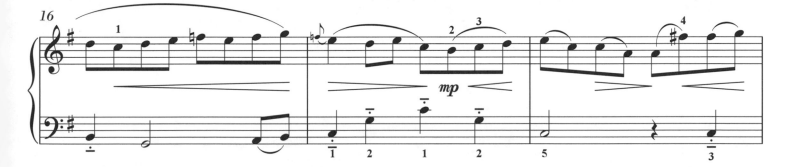

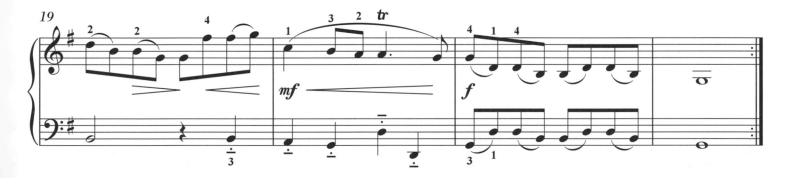

Cantabile in F Major

Georg Philipp Telemann

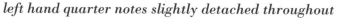

left hand quarter notes slightly detached throughout

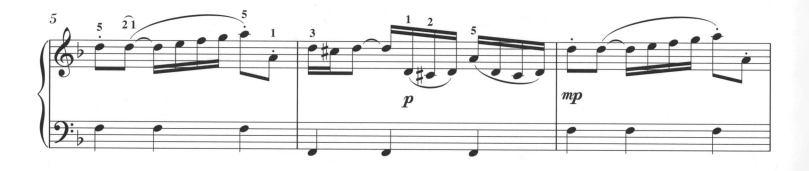

Fingering by Elena Abend.
Tempo, articulations and dynamics are editorial suggestions.

Copyright © 2014 by G. Schirmer, Inc. (ASCAP) New York, NY
International Copyright Secured. All Rights Reserved.

14

17

21

25

28

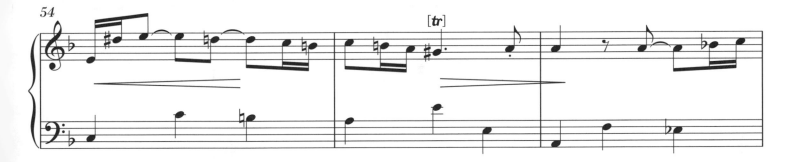

Tambourin
from Harpsichord Pieces

Jean-Philippe Rameau

Fingering by Matthew Edwards.
Tempo, articulation and dynamics are stylistic editorial suggestions. Trills begin on the note above.

Copyright © 2014 by G. Schirmer, Inc. (ASCAP) New York, NY
International Copyright Secured. All Rights Reserved.

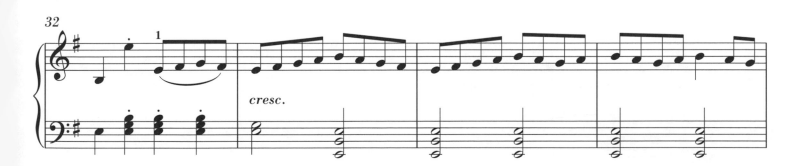

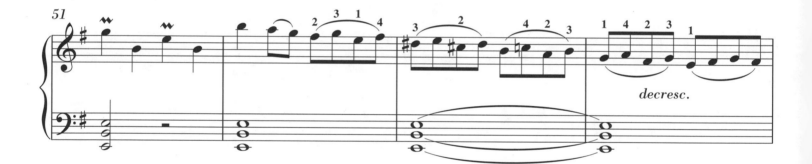

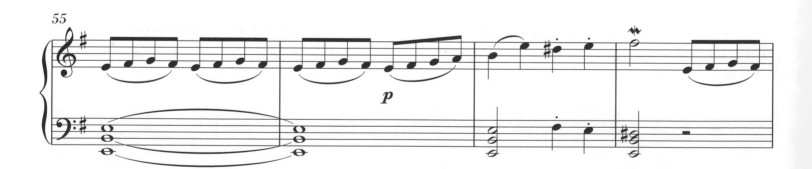

LABORUM
DULCE
LENIMEN

G. SCHIRMER

Dance Suite No. 2 in F Major
I

Georg Philipp Telemann

GAVOTTE
Allegro moderato

left hand quarter notes slightly detached throughout

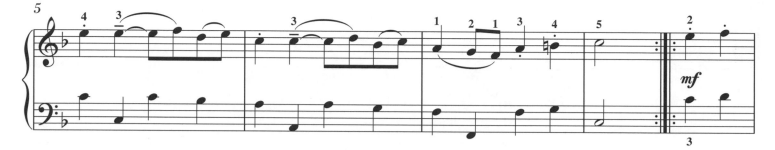

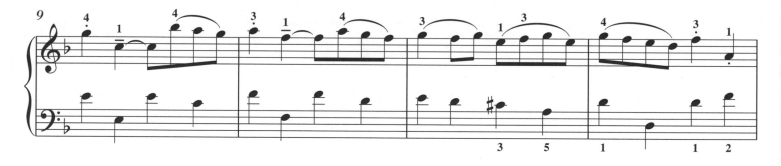

Fingering by Stefanie Jacob.
Tempo, dynamics, and articulations are stylistic editorial suggestions. Trill begins on the note above.
No repeats on the *Da Capo*.

Copyright © 2014 by G. Schirmer, Inc. (ASCAP) New York, NY
International Copyright Secured. All Rights Reserved.

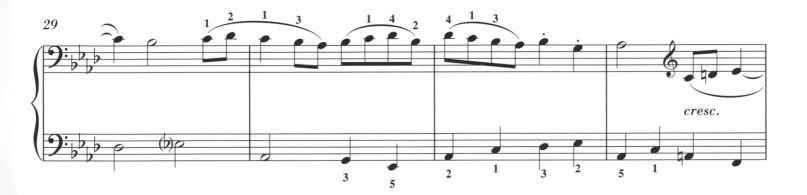

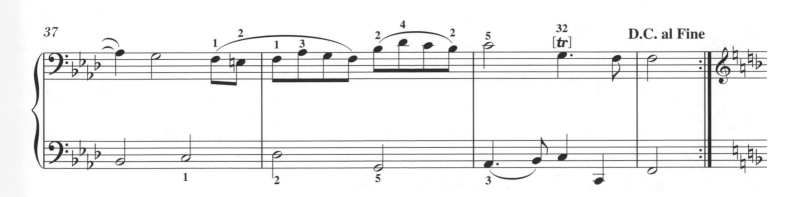

30

SARABANDE

II

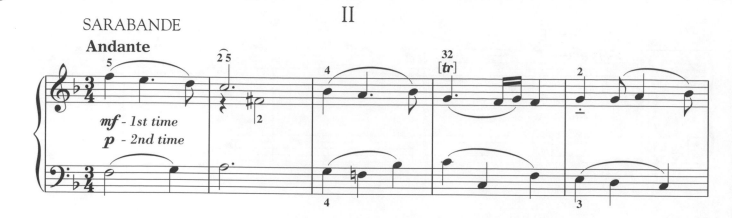

Ornaments have been realized for this edition. Articulations and dynamics are editorial suggestions.

III

BOURRÉE

left hand half notes slightly detached throughout

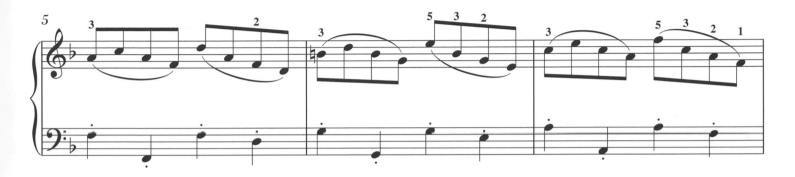

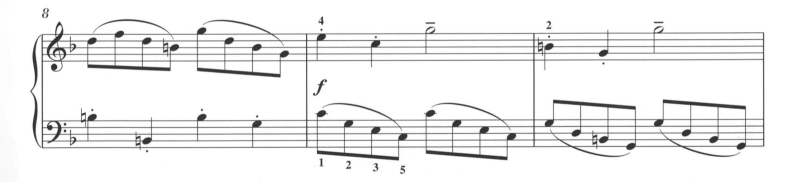

Articulations and dynamics are editorial suggestions.

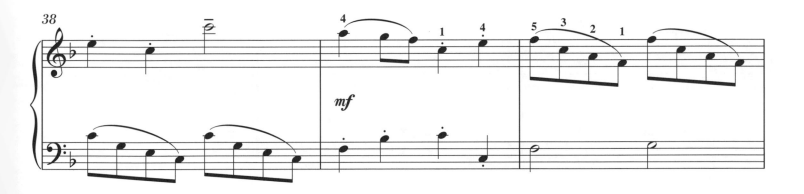

Prelude in G Major

from *Suite de pièce*, Volume 2, No. 9

George Frideric Handel
HWV 442

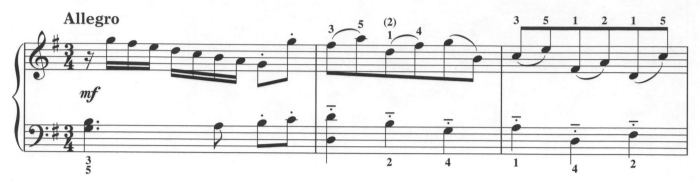

Fingering by Jeannie Yu.
Articulations and dynamics are stylistic editorial suggestions.

Copyright © 2014 by G. Schirmer, Inc. (ASCAP) New York, NY
International Copyright Secured. All Rights Reserved.

Lament
(La Gémissante)
from the Second Suite of Harpsichord Pieces, Book 1

Jean-François Dandrieu

Fingering by Elena Abend.
The ornamentation for this piece has been omitted for this edition. Tempo, dynamics and articulations are stylistic editorial suggestions. Trills begin on the second note above. Repeat of the first section is optional in performance.

Copyright © 2014 by G. Schirmer, Inc. (ASCAP) New York, NY
International Copyright Secured. All Rights Reserved.

Sonata in D minor

Domenico Scarlatti
L. 423 (K. 32, P. 14)

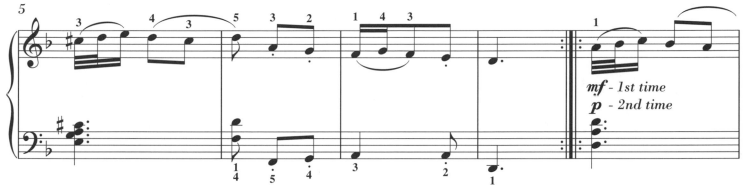

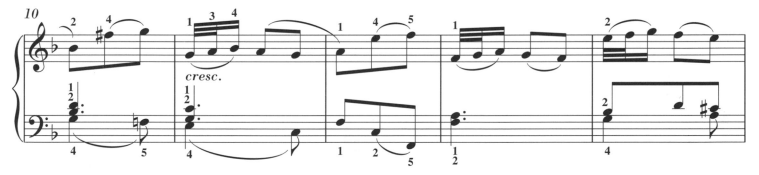

Fingering by Jeannie Yu.
Tempo, articulations and dynamics are stylistic editorial suggestions. Ornaments have been realized for this edition.

Copyright © 2014 by G. Schirmer, Inc. (ASCAP) New York, NY
International Copyright Secured. All Rights Reserved.

Bourrée

from Lute Suite No. 1 in E minor

Johann Sebastian Bach
BWV 996

[Allegro moderato]

left hand quarter notes slightly detached throughout

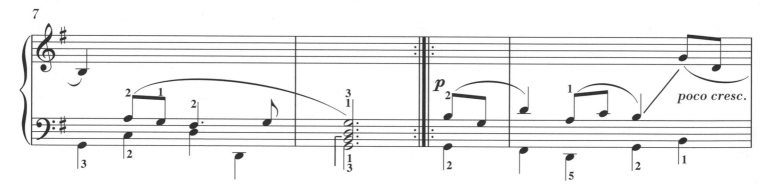

Edited and with fingering by Christos Tsitsaros.
Tempo, articulations and dynamics are editorial suggestions. Bach indicated none of these details in his manuscript.

Copyright © 2009 by G. Schirmer, Inc. (ASCAP), New York, NY
International Copyright Secured. All Rights Reserved.

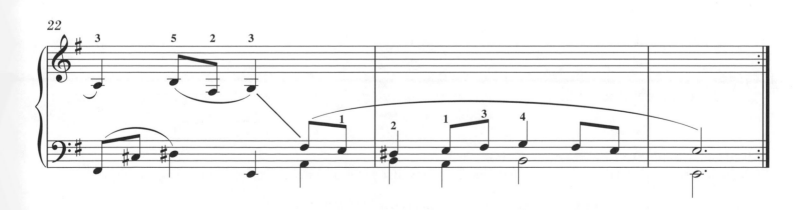

Sonata in G Major

Domenico Scarlatti
L. 79 (K. 391, P. 364)

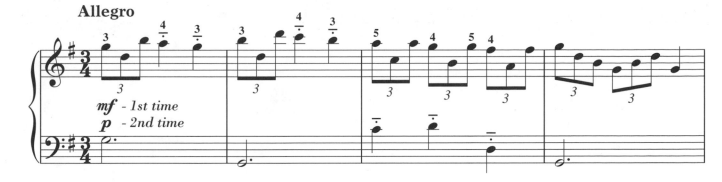

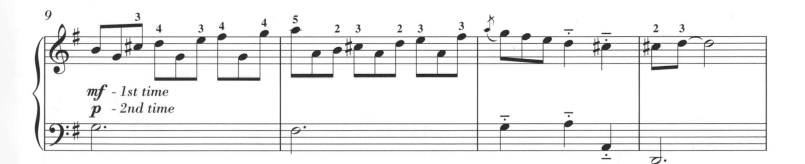

Fingering by Jeannie Yu.
Articulation and dynamics are stylistic editorial suggestions. Trills begin on the note above.

Copyright © 2014 by G. Schirmer, Inc. (ASCAP) New York, NY
International Copyright Secured. All Rights Reserved.

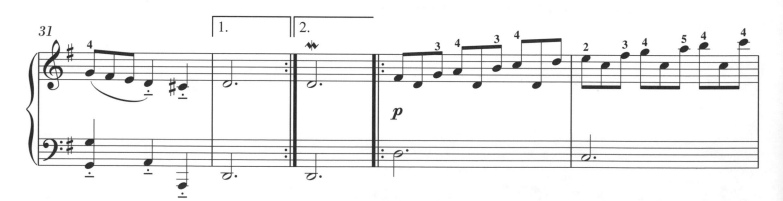

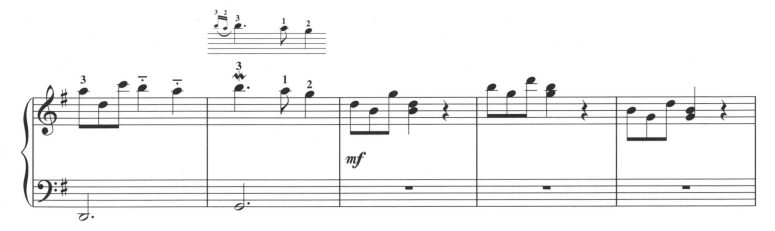

Prelude in C minor

Johann Sebastian Bach
BWV 999

[Allegro moderato]

Edited and with fingering by Christos Tsitsaros.
Editorial suggestions appear in brackets.

Copyright © 2012 by G. Schirmer, Inc. (ASCAP) New York, NY
International Copyright Secured. All Rights Reserved.

LABORUM
DULCE
LENIMEN

G. SCHIRMER

Allegro
from Suite in G minor

George Frideric Handel
HWV 432

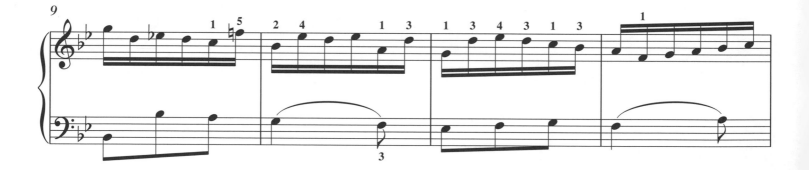

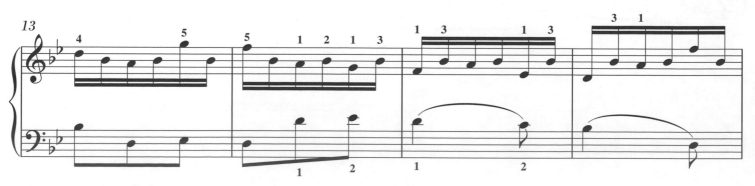

Fingering by Jeannie Yu.
Articulations and dynamics are stylistic editorial suggestions. Trills begin on the note above.

Copyright © 2014 by G. Schirmer, Inc. (ASCAP) New York, NY
International Copyright Secured. All Rights Reserved.

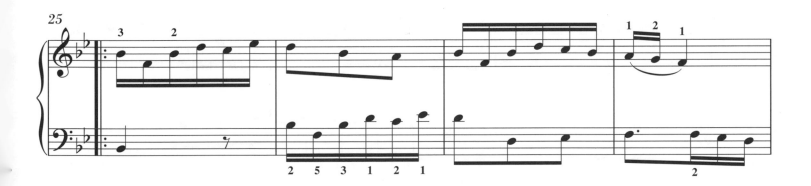

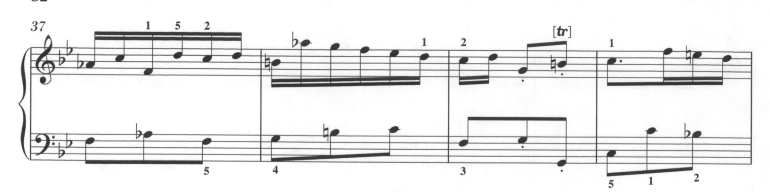

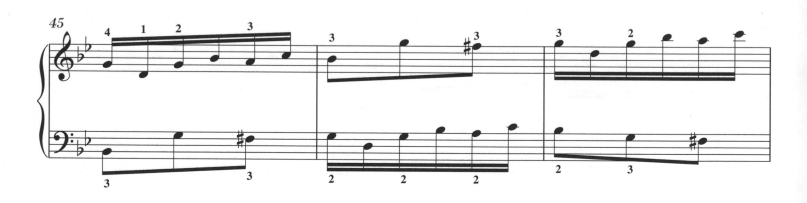

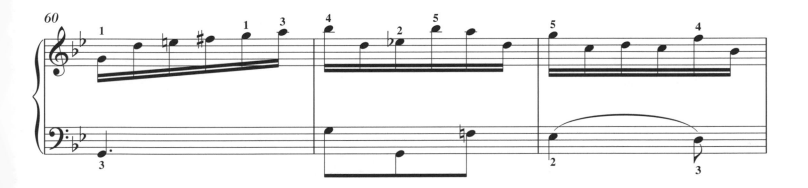

The Little Trifle

(Le Petit-Rien)
from the fourteenth order of Harpsichord Pieces

François Couperin

Fingering by Jeannie Yu.
Dynamics and articulations are stylistic editorial suggestions. Ornamentation, which may be omitted to make the piece easier, is integral to the French Baroque style. An alternative would be to omit only left hand ornaments.

Copyright © 2014 by G. Schirmer, Inc. (ASCAP) New York, NY
International Copyright Secured. All Rights Reserved.

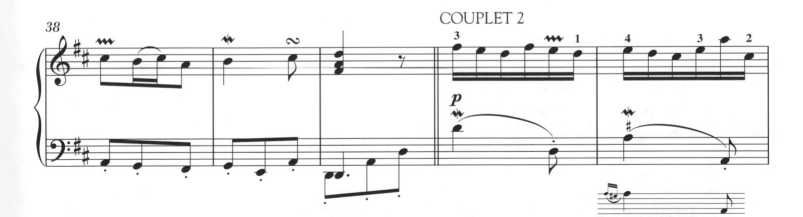

COUPLET 2

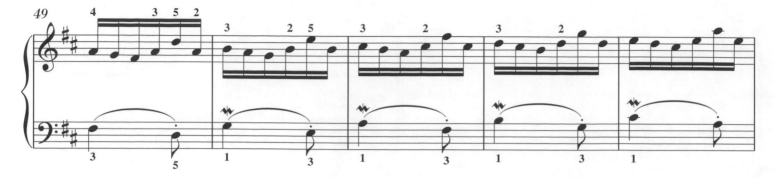

Prelude in F Major

Johann Sebastian Bach
BWV 927

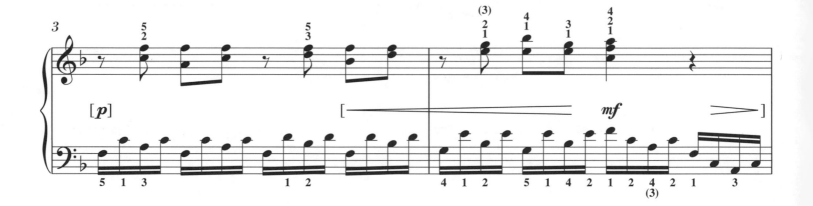

Edited and with fingering by Christos Tsitsaros.
Editorial suggestions are in brackets.

Copyright © 2012 by G. Schirmer, Inc. (ASCAP) New York, NY
International Copyright Secured. All Rights Reserved.

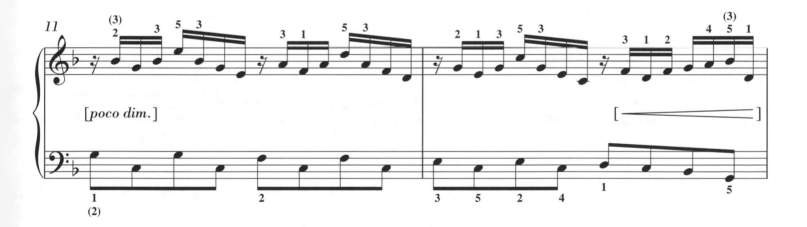

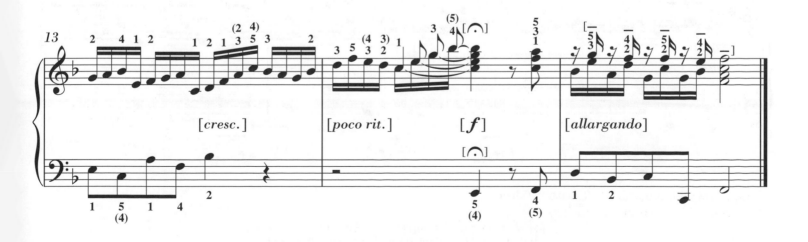

Prelude in D minor

Johann Sebastian Bach
BWV 926

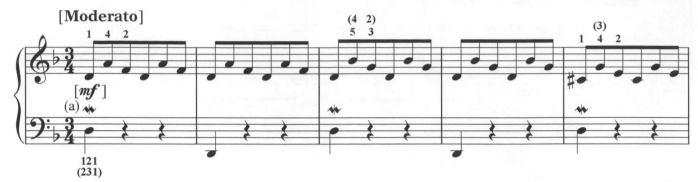

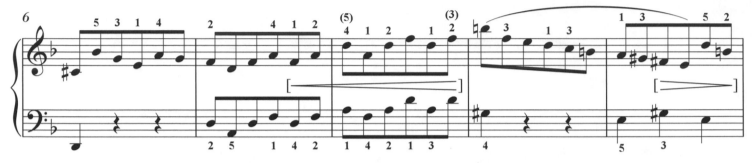

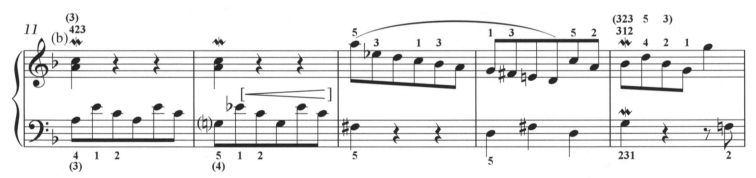

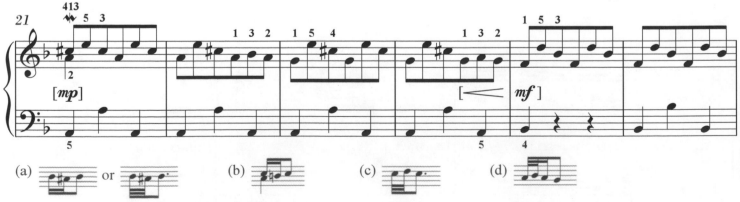

Edited and with fingering by Christos Tsitsaros.
Editorial suggestions are in brackets.

Copyright © 2012 by G. Schirmer, Inc. (ASCAP) New York, NY
International Copyright Secured. All Rights Reserved.

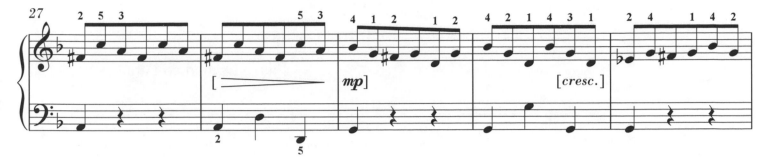

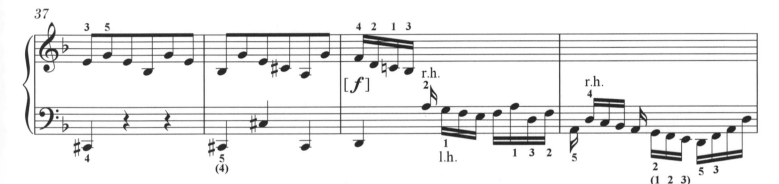

Toccata
from Sonata No. 6 in A Major

Pietro Domenico Paradies [Paradisi]

Fingering by Stefanie Jacob.

Tempo and dynamics are stylistic editorial suggestions. Play eighth notes, in right or left hand, slightly detached throughout.

Copyright © 2014 by G. Schirmer, Inc. (ASCAP) New York, NY
International Copyright Secured. All Rights Reserved.

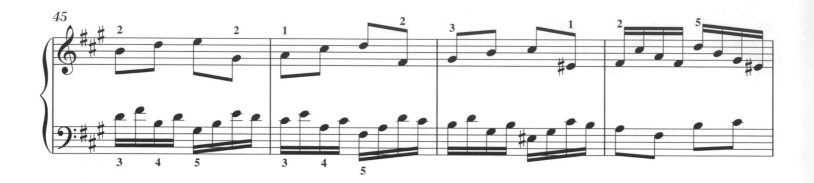

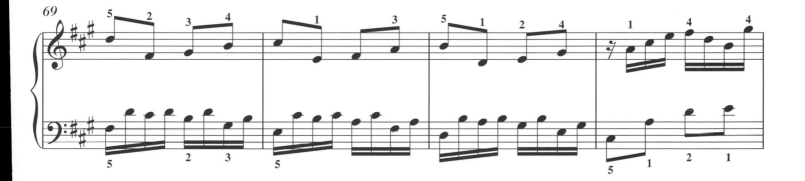

ABOUT THE EDITOR

RICHARD WALTERS

Richard Walters is a pianist, composer, and editor of hundred of publications in a long music publishing career. He is Vice President of Classical Publications at Hal Leonard, and directs a variety of publications for piano, voice, and solo instruments. Walters directs all publishing in the Schirmer Performance Editions series. Among other piano publications, he is editor of the revised edition of *Samuel Barber: Complete Piano Music*, *Leonard Bernstein: Music for Piano*, and the multi-volume series *The World's Great Classical Music*. His editing credits for vocal publications include *Samuel Barber: 65 Songs*, *Benjamin Britten: Collected Songs*, *Benjamin Britten: Complete Folksong Arrangements*, *Leonard Bernstein: Art Songs and Arias*, *The Purcell Collection: Realizations by Benjamin Britten*, *Bernstein Theatre Songs*, *G. Schirmer Collection of American Art Song*, *28 Italian Songs and Arias for the Seventeenth and Eighteenth Centuries*, 80 volumes of standard repertoire in the Vocal Library series, and the multi-volume *The Singer's Musical Theatre Anthology*. Walters has published dozens of various arrangements, particularly for voice and piano, and is the composer of nine song cycles. He was educated with a bachelor's degree in piano at Simpson College, where he studied piano with Robert Larsen and composition with Sven Lekberg, and graduate studies in composition at the University of Minnesota, where he studied with Dominick Argento.